the
International

Dictionary
of
Derivatives

2nd edition

WITHDRAWN
UTSA Libraries

D0731492

GLOBAL
professional
publishing

© Global Professional Publishing Ltd 2009

Apart from any fair dealing for the purpose of research or private study, or criticism or review, as permitted under the Copyright, Designs and Patents Act 1988, this publication may only be reproduced, stored or transmitted, in any form or by any means, with the prior permission in writing of the publisher, or in the case of reprographic reproduction in accordance with the terms and licences issued by the Copyright Licensing Agency. Enquiries concerning reproduction outside those terms should be addressed to the publisher. The address is below:

Global Professional Publishing Ltd
Random Acres
Slip Mill Lane
Hawkhurst
Cranbrook
Kent TN18 5AD
Email: publishing@gppbooks.com

Global Professional Publishing believes that the sources of information upon which the book is based are reliable, and has made every effort to ensure the complete accuracy of the text. However, neither Global Professional Publishing, the authors nor any contributors can accept any legal responsibility whatsoever for consequences that may aise from errors or omissions or any opinion or advice given.

ISBN 978-1-906403-05-8

Printed by Replika Press, India

For full details of Global Professional Publishing titles in Finance, Banking and Management see our website at:
www.gppbooks.com

Library
University of Texas
at San Antonio

Preface

The definitions given in The International Dictionary of Derivatives are, as far as I'm aware, those most commonly accepted by derivatives practitioners around the world. They may not be the ones used by every derivatives desk in every company, but they do represent a consensus.

In the dictionary's compilation I've discovered many regional differences even when the same language is involved such as between LIFFE and CBOT. Some are quite astounding, and I'm sure must lead to an increased transaction risk. Indeed, several words have almost as many definitions as there are different ways of constructing synthetics!

The end result is a dictionary which is not intended to be the font of all knowledge regarding derivatives. But neither is it meant to be a work of fiction. So, if you spot a mistake, think the dictionary could be improved by changing a definition or wish to add something new, please let me know at the address on the opposite page or email me at sales@takethat.co.uk. If your comments are taken on-board we'll send you a free copy of the next edition of the dictionary, or another of TTL's titles.

Alex Kiam

A

ABB
Association des Banques Belges

ABI
Association of British Insurers
Association of Italian Bankers

ABS
Asset-Backed Security

AE
Account Executive

AFBD
Association of Futures Brokers and Dealers

AFOF
Authorised Futures and Options Funds

AMEX
American Stock Exchange

AOM
Australian Options Market

AON
All Or None

AP
Associated Person

APT
Automated Pit Trading system

ASB
The Accounting Standards Board

ASXD
Australian Stock Exchange Derivatives

ATM
At-The-Money

ATS
Automated Trade System

Accreting Swap
A Swap in which the notional principle or actual principle is increased by an agreed amount each period over the life of the Swap. The opposite of an amortising Swap.

Accrual Option
Sometimes called a corridor or fairway option. This option gives the holder the right to receive daily interest when the underlying asset price trades within a specified range. The maximum "payout" is the amount repaid on an accrual option if the asset trades within the specified range on each day of the accrual period. So the amount received upon expiry is calculated as:

Settlement amount =

$$\left(\frac{\text{number of accrual days}}{\text{total days in accrual period}} \right) \times \text{maximum pay-out}$$

Accrual Period
The period during which an asset price is monitored to determine the payout of an accrual option

AC/DC Option
An option where the purchaser can choose for it to be either a call option or a put option.

Active Risk
The risk incurred by an investment manager when he tries to add value to a portfolio relative to the benchmark. It is a direct function of the extent to which individual financial assets are weighted within a portfolio differently from their weighting in an index. A portfolio which contains assets with exactly the same weighting as in an index such as the FTSE 100 will have zero active risk.

Accounting Principles
The accounting treatment of derivatives are governed by four basic accounting concepts:
accrual, consistency, going concern, and prudence.

Act-of-God Bond
See catastrophe bond

Actuals
The physical or cash commodity being traded, as opposed to the commodity futures contract.

AGARCH
Asymmetric GARCH. This variation of the GARCH model is appropriate when you expect more volatility following a market fall than after a market rise (such as the equity markets).

Aggregation

The policy under which all derivatives positions owned or controlled by a single trader or group of traders are combined to determine reporting status and speculative limit compliance.

American Depository Receipt

A receipt which indicates a claim on any number of shares in foreign corporations that a depository bank holds on behalf of American investors.

American-Style Option

An option that may be exercised at any time up to and including the expiry date. These options allow the holder to take notional profits (or losses) at any stage.

Amortising Swap

A Swap in which the notional principal is reduced by an agreed amount each period over the lifetime of the Swap. These transactions can be used to hedge borrowings in which a proportion of the principal needs to be repaid in addition to interest.

Anti-Dilution Clause

A clause which allows the exercise price of a warrant to be adjusted to take into account any stock splits, dividends or rights issues which may be made by the issuing company.

Arbitrage

1. The simultaneous purchase of a derivative at a low price in one market and selling at a higher price in another, thus making a risk-free profit.

2. The purchase of a derivative at a low price in the market when higher prices are being asked.
3. A spread trade where the derivative bought at the low price is different from the one sold at the higher price (the proceeds from the sale being used for the purchase).

Arbitration
A forum for impartial settlement of disputes often convened by regularity organisations in the derivatives industry.

Asian Option
The holder of an Asian option receives the difference between the exercise price and the average price of the underlying financial instrument during the life of the contract. Particularly useful for currency hedging where it is used as a "one stop" method to hedge the price risk of regular transactions (sales or purchases) of a constant amount of currency.

Ask
The price at which a market-maker is ready to sell. The "ask" will usually exceed the "bid" and the bid-ask spread represents the profit made by a market-maker when turning round one unit of a derivative. It is also known as the "offer price".

Asset-Backed Bond
A bond that is also an asset-backed security.

Asset-Backed Security
This is a fixed income security that pays its coupon and principal from a specified revenue stream and also has a specific asset as collateral.

Asset Swap
A Swap that converts a floating coupon asset into a fixed coupon asset, or vice versa.

Assignment
When a new counterparty replaces one of the originals in a Swap. In effect, the sale of a Swap contract.

Associated Person
An individual who solicits orders, customers, or funds on behalf of parties who are registered with regulating authorities of the market.

At-the-Money Forward
When the strike price equals that of the forward price.

At-the-Money Option
An option is "at the money" if its strike price is equal to the spot price.

Atlantic Spread
Going long in an American option and short in an otherwise identical European option, or vice versa. This allows exploitation of the time value of options.

Automatic Exercise
A trader can arrange for any put/call options whose exercise prices are more than a pre-specified amount above/below the spot price to be automatically exercised. This facility is not offered by all markets, but it allows traders who forget they are holding in-the-money options to realise their profits.

Average Price Option
An option whose underlying price is an average over time of a certain risk factor.

Average Rate Option
Pays the difference between the average of prices recorded over a specified period and a specified strike price. The

expiry date is usually the same as the last recording date used to determine the average. A form of Asian option.

Average Strike Option

Pays the difference between the asset price on the expiry date and the average of the asset prices recording over a specified period. The expiry date is often set to be later than the last recording date of the average. A form of Asian option.

B

BBA
British Bankers Association

BBAISR
British Bankers Association Interest Settlement Rate

BBF
Bolsa Brasiliera de Futuros

BCC
Banque Centrale de Compensation

BELFOX
Belgium Futures and Options Exchange

BFE
Baltic Futures Exchange

BFI
Baltic Freight Index

BIS
Bank for International Settlements

BOBL
Bundesobligation (German Government five year bonds)

BOJ
Bank of Japan

BSE
Bombay Stock Exchange

BTAN
Bons du Trésor à Intéret Annuel Normalisé

BUND
Bundesanleihen (German Federal Government Bonds)

Back-To-Back Loan
Two companies make loans to one another in different currencies and possibly with different interest rates attached to them but with the same expiry date. This simple transaction is basically an on-balance sheet Swap as each counterparty must carry the principal loan value on its balance sheet as a risk asset.

Backwardation
Backwardation occurs when the spot rate in any market is more expensive than the forward rate. These situations usually occur in the commodities markets when there is a temporary shortage of a particular commodity. For example the markets may be expecting an excellent wheat harvest for the year but weather conditions may be preventing the producers getting into the fields. So there will be a temporary shortage of wheat and the spot prices will be high, whereas the forward rate will be low since the markets know a large volume of wheat will be eventually produced.

Barrier Options
The value of barrier options at maturity depends on the value of the underlying financial instrument at maturity and on the trade prices between inception and expiry. If the underlying financial instrument reaches the "barrier" during the life of the option one rule is used to calculate the value at expiry. If the barrier is not reached, another rule applies.

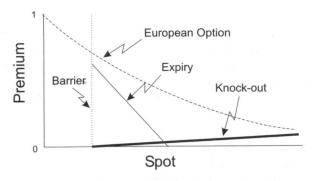

Option Premium as a Function of Spot
(Down & Out Put)

Barrier-European Combinations
Strategies involving European options that are adapted to use barrier options in one or both legs.For example risk renewals, synthetic forwards, spreads and strangles.

Basis
1. The reference point from which calculations are made.
2. The difference between the cash price of an underlying financial instrument and the futures price for the same instrument.

Basis Point
One hundredth of one percent of the principal amount or notional value.

Basis Risk
The risk of a relative change occurring in the price relationship between the hedged item and the hedge. The basis may increase or decrease depending on the relative demand for the underlying financial instrument and the related future. Although the scope for movement is limited by the possibility of cash and carry arbitrage

---

(arbitrage activity will correct the market) there can still be significant fluctuations of the basis. Basis traders seek to take advantage of these fluctuations by charting the limit of divergence and then buying or selling when they expect reversal to take place.

Basis Swap

A series of payments which vary over time according to some agreed calculation basis for a different set of payments which also vary over time according to a separate method of calculation or schedule of payment. In other words the reference rates for both sides of the Swap are floating but are calculated from different bases. Example:

	US Dollar Floating Rate Payments	US Dollar Floating Rate Receipts
1/1/2008	6m Libor	
1/7/2008	6m Libor	12m Libor
1/1/2009	6m Libor	
1/7/2009	6m Libor	12m Libor

Basis Trading

The purchase or sale of a financial instrument and the simultaneous sale or purchase of the instruments futures contract. The basis trade is an essential part of cash and carry (and reverse cash and carry) arbitrage.

Basle Committee

The Basle Committee was set up in 1974 by governors representing the central banks of the G10 nations in an effort to establish a set of international standards on bank supervision. Amongst other things it suggested risk weightings for on-and-off-balance sheet instruments, giving off-balance sheet derivative transactions a risk weighting of 50%.

Bear Market
One in which prices show a generally downward trend. The opposite of a bull market.

Bear Spread
The purchase of put options in a financial instrument at a given strike price and a simultaneous writing of put options for the same instrument and same expiry date at a lower strike price. The overall effect of this strategy represents a bearish outlook on the instrument concerned.

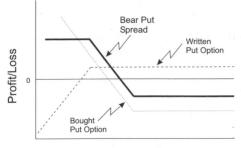

Benchmark
The "zero level" or "neutral point" against which financial risk or performance are measured. Risk quantification against a benchmark is at the centre of all activities for traders, market-makers and portfolio managers. It is the out-performance of a benchmark by a portfolio manager, through the acceptance of risk, that creates worth.

Best-of-Two Option
A return which equals the maximum of two option returns. For example the maximum of a call on financial instrument A and a put on financial instrument B.

Bet Option
A binary option.

Beta
A measure of market risk. It is defined as:-
$$\text{Beta} = \beta = (\sigma_p \times \sigma_{p,m})/\sigma_m$$
Where σp is the return volatility of the portfolio, σm is the return volatility of the market, and $\sigma p,m$ is their correlation values. The expected excess return for your portfolio above the risk free rate is simply your portfolio's beta multiplied by the expected excess return of the market portfolio.

Bid
The price at which a market-maker is ready to buy. (See *Ask*)

Binary Option
The holder receives the right to a pre-specified currency amount if the price of an underlying financial instrument progresses beyond the strike price at the expiry date. Binary options are also known as bets or digital options and are quoted per unit of currency.

Black, Derman and Toy
An interest rate option model which uses arbitrage-free computation lattices for the evaluation of interest rate options.

Black-Scholes Formula
A formula developed by Fischer Black and Myron Scholes for the pricing of call options. The basic Black-Scholes model was developed in 1973 and has been the pathfinder for virtually all pricing models developed since then. Like all ground-breaking equations it requires some quite limiting assumptions:
✔   the option is only exerciseable at expiration
✔   the market is continuous
✔   no dividend is payable over the lifetime of the option
✔   the risk-free rate of interest is constant
✔   there are no taxes, costs or bid-ask spreads

✔   the underlying can be shorted without penalty
✔   prices are continous and not subject to step-like changes

Bond Future
A long-term interest rate future. A standard contract that entitles the holder to a specified number of Government bonds on a specified date in the future. The underlying is a notional bond with standardised features allowing the contract specifications to remain constant.

Bond Option
Options on bond futures give the owner the right but not the obligation to buy or sell a bond future up to or on a specified date.

Bonus issue
A method of reducing the relative price of a stock by issuing cost-free shares to existing stockholders. For example, if a share is trading around £20, then a "one for one" bonus issue will result in the share trading at around £10. This is intended to make dealing more manageable and has a consequent effect on options.

Box Spread
An option structure equivalent to a zero coupon bond. The trader longs the market at a strike price P_1 and shorts the market at a strike price P_2 via calls and puts with the same expiry date. The value is given by the present value of $P_1 - P_2$.

Boosted Coupon Note
The investor receives an enhanced coupon for the number of days during which an equity index stays within a certain range by selling strips of binary options on an equity index.

Borrowing Arbitrage
When assets or liabilities can be swapped from one interest

rate basis in one currency to another basis in the same or a different currency. For example a fixed rate annual bond may be swapped with a floating rate to create a more attractive cost of borrowing.

Brady Commission

US Treasury Secretary Nicholas Brady headed a presidential task force on market mechanisms to investigate the causes of the October 1987 stock market crash. The report showed that liquidity in the market was insufficient to cope with the pressures created by large institutional sellers. Various position, price and volume limits were recommended as "circuit breakers" to prevent similar crashes in the future.

Brady Bond

Bonds resulting from a debt restructuring and where the redemption value of at least some of the bonds (resulting from the restructuring) has been guaranteed by the US Treasury.

Break Forward

A forward contract with a cancellation feature built in. A purchaser has the option to pay a cancellation premium and complete the contract in the spot market, or to complete the contract in the forward market.

Breakout

When the price of a financial instrument departs from its current behaviour pattern defined by resistance and support levels on a chart. Breakout occurs when a behaviour pattern indicates the formation of a new trend.

Brokerage

A fee charged by a broker for executing a transaction.

Brundle
A strip of consecutive quarterly Eurodollar or Euroyen futures contracts.

Bucketing
The illegal practice of accepting orders to buy or sell and not executing those orders. Also the illegal use of a customers margin deposit.

Bull Market
One in which prices show a generally upward trend.

Bull Spread
The opposite to a bear spread. A bull spread incorporates the purchase of call options at a given strike price and writing the same number of calls on the same underlying financial instrument with the same expiry date but at a higher strike price. This form of options strategy indicates a bullish outlook on the market.

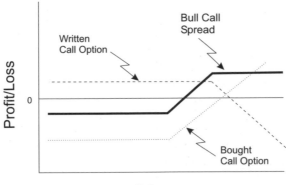

Bullet Maturity
A bond which only pays interest periodically, and repays the entire principal upon maturity.

Butterfly Spread

A strategy involving a trader selling a straddle and simultaneously buying a strangle on the same financial instrument for the same maturity.

It is used in a situation where low volatility is expected and a trader can expect a profit from the premiums received less those paid for the strangle. If however the price does prove volatile a strangle provides some form of protection against the potentially unlimited losses involved with writing a straddle.

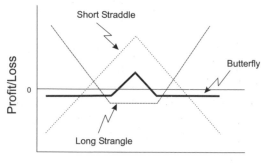

Price

Buy-Back Clause

Most over-the-counter derivatives are designed to be held for maturity, but those with a Buy-Back Clause may be unwound as part of the contract agreement.

Buy-Write Strategy

Involves buying a share and then selling an at-the-money call option. This strategy is bearish in outlook with lower downside losses as the share price falls.

Buying Hedge

Buying futures contracts to protect against the possible increased costs of a commodity required for future use.

CAC
Compagnie des Agents de Change

CAD
Capital Adequacy Directive

CAPM
Capital Asset Pricing Model

CBOE
Chicago Board Options Exchange

CBOT
Chicago Board of Trade

CCC
Commodity Credit Corporation

CD
Certificate of Deposit

CDR
Collateralised Depositry Receipt

C&F
Cost and Freight

CFD
Contract for Difference

CFO
Cancel Former Order

CFTC
Commodites Futures Trading Commission

CHAPS
Clearing House Automated Payments System

CHIPS
Clearing House Interbank Payment System

CIBOR
Copenhagen Interbank Offered Rate

CIF
Cost, Insurance and Freight

CME
Chicago Mercantile Exchange

CMO
Collateralised Mortgage Obligation

COMEX
Commodity Exchange

CPO
Commodity Pool Operator

CPS
Clearing Processing System

CRB
Commodity Research Bureau

CSCE
Coffee, Sugar and Coco Exchange

CTA
Commodity Trading Advisor

Calculation Agent
A third party given the responsibility for ensuring the correct calculation of payment for derivative contracts.

Calendar Spread
The sale and purchase of put or call options in a same financial instrument and at the same striking price but for different maturity dates. This strategy is used in stable markets to exploit the time value element of options.

Call Option
The right, but not obligation, to buy an underlying financial instrument at a specified price on or before the expiration date.

Call Ratio Back Spread
The purchase of two or more call options at one strike price and the sale of one call option at a lower strike price. The multiple options will usually be out-of-the-money, and the single call option will usually be in-the-money. The strategy as a whole should be delta-neutral and the strike prices selected accordingly.

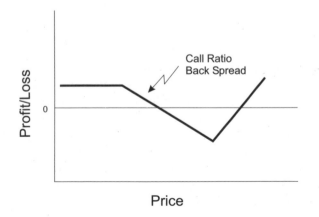

Call Ratio Spread

The sale of two or more call options at one strike price and the purchase of a call option at a lower strike price. The strategy as a whole should be delta-neutral, and the strike price is selected accordingly.

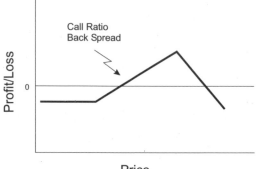

Callable Swap

Contracts may be terminated at the buyer's (fixed rate payer) discretion without a financial penalty.

Cap

An OTC instrument which ensures a maximum interest rate over a defined period. Equivalent to buying a strip of interest rate call options at the same strike price but with sequential expiry dates.

Capital Asset Pricing Model

Developed by James Tobin and Bill Sharp in the 1960's, the CAPM treats the risk inherent in any financial instrument as being made up of two components: Specific risk and market risk (systematic risk). According to the CAPM, financial markets will compensate investors for taking market risk but not for taking on specific risk. This is because specific risk can be diversified away and no one should expect to be compensated for carrying unnecessary risk. In the CAPM, market risk is measured using "beta ".

Capital Guarantee Structure
An investment where the final value has a guaranteed minimum, created with zero coupon bond and option spreads.

Caplet
An interest rate option to pay fixed interest in a Forward Rate Agreement.

Caption
An option to buy a Cap.

Carrying Broker
A member of a commodity exchange to whom customers choose to clear their trades.

Cash and Carry Arbitrage
Used to exploit a situation by borrowing cash to buy a physical commodity and simultaneously sell a future. Used when the future price is higher than the spot price of the underlying instrument plus the interest cost of borrowing the necessary cash until the future becomes deliverable.

Cash Commodity
Actual stocks of a commodity available for immediate delivery within a short specified period (as opposed to futures).

Catastrophe Bond
A bond that receives a lower coupon, and perhaps principal, after a catastrophe has occurred. The possible catastrophes, such as earthquakes, hurricanes, and tornadoes, will be specified as will a geographical region. Also known as Cat Bonds.

Ceiling
A Cap

Certificate of Deposit
A cross between a bond and a traditional savings account. A depositor's money is placed in an account and kept there until the certificate matures.

Certificated Stock
Stock of a commodity that has been inspected and proven to be of such quality as to be deliverable against futures contracts.

Cheapest to deliver
Bond futures contracts use notional bonds as their underlying assets. The precise terms attached to these notional bonds are usually not matched by an actual bond. Thus, the "cheapest to deliver" is the actual bond whose price gives the seller the greatest return when he buys it in order to deliver. The exchanges on which bond futures are traded publish a list of actual bonds which are acceptable for settlement of a bond futures contract.

Chooser Options
Similar to a straddle in that a buyer purchases a call and a put with the same strike and expiry. However, unlike a straddle, he must make a choice on a specified date prior to expiry as to which option he will exercise. Usually this will be the most valuable on the specified date but may not be if the owner considers that the direction of the market will mean the other option ending up being more profitable.

Christmas Tree Spread
The use of six options at four strike prices to help limit risk.

Churning
Over trading of an account by a broker who has control of trading decisions for that account in order to make more commission while ignoring the interests of the customer.

Circus Swap
Combined Interest Rate and Currency Swap. The exchange of interest payments on a principal sum in two different currencies with one set of payments made at a floating rate and the other at a fixed rate.

Clean Risk
The risk to which an individual, corporation or institution is exposed when a contract matures and it pays out according to its own obligations before it is certain that payment by the counterparty will be met. Includes the failure to make swap differential payments on time, failure to deliver the correct financial instrument, and failure to deliver it to the correct location. Most errors represented by "clean risk" are caused by error rather than fraud.

Clearing
The procedure for which trades are checked for accuracy.

Clearing House
The central office where commodity exchange transactions are settled. The clearing house ensures prompt settlement of contracts by standing in as the counterparty to both buyer and seller.

Clearing House Automated Payments System (CHAPS)
A computerised system for clearing cheques. Known as the Clearing House Interbank Payment System (CHIPS) in the USA.

Clearing Member
A member of a futures exchange who is also a member of the clearing house. Any and all trades made on a particular exchange must be settled through one of its clearing members.

Close
The end of the trading session.

Collateralised Mortgage Obligations
A form of mortgage-backed security where the bonds are secured on a portfolio of mortgages. The sum over all tranches of the CMO interest payouts must be equal to the sum over all mortgages of interest payments

Collar
Allows the holder of a Cap or a Floor to hedge their interest rate exposure. In a collar some of the upside potential is relinquished in return for a lower cost compared to the price of a Cap or Floor on its own. For example, if a fund manager has money in variable rate investments and wants to protect its income it will by a Floor. But instead of paying the full premium it will simultaneously sell a Cap. This then effectively creates a "collar" around its variable rate investments.

Commodity
An item of trade or commerce, including services or rights, in which contracts for future delivery may be traded or exchanged.

Commodity Future
A futures contract whose underlying asset is a physical commodity.

Commodity Linked Bond
Also known as an embedded commodity option which is a zero coupon bond (paying no interest before maturity) whose redemption value is linked to the price of a commodity.

Commodity Option
If you buy a commodity option call (put) you have the right, but not the obligation, to take a long (short) position in the commodities market at a specific price on or before a specified date.

Commodity Swap
A Swap in which the floating rate is linked to the price of a specific commodity. It is an over-the-counter product that is tailored for the specific requirements of each individual hedger.

Comparative Advantage
When a trader or a company has the capacity to borrow funds in a particular market at a preferential rate to those they are dealing with or competing against.

Compound Option
A compound option gives the holder the right, but not an obligation, to enter into an option at a specified rate at a future date. It is, in effect, an option on an option. It is primarily used by companies who wish to hedge against a risk to which they may become exposed. For instance a company tendering for a foreign contract could, if they won the contract, require an option to hedge its currency exposure. A compound option allows it to hedge the "potential" currency exposure without paying a large premium for the underlying option for which it may have no requirement if it does not win the contract.

Condor Spread
The sale of a strangle and simultaneous purchase of another strangle with the same maturity and on the same underlying asset but with its two legs further out-of-the-money. (pto).

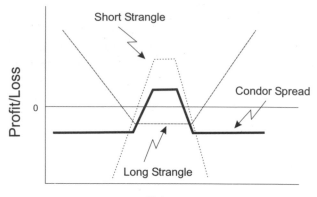

Price

Consolidation

A period in trading activity during which prices move sideways. Traders will be evaluating their positions during periods of consolidation while waiting for the next market move.

Contango

Also known as forwardation, it is a situation on commodity markets when the spot price is lower than the forward price. This is a normal situation, where the forward price reflects the cost-of-carry as opposed to backwardation.

Contingent Option

The buyer of a contingent option only pays a premium when it is exercised. This obviously only takes place if the option is in-the-money at expiry. Naturally the premiums are higher than for standard options.

Contract for Difference

An over-the-counter contract where the price for delivery of the financial instrument at a future date is fixed in advance and the counterparty pays the difference between the agreed price and the market price.

Contract Grades
Grades of commodities that must be met when delivering cash commodities against futures contracts. These grades are listed in the rules of exchanges and are accompanied by a schedule of discounts and premiums which can be applied for the delivery of a commodity which varies from the contract grade.

Contract Month
The month in which a futures contract must be delivered.

Conversion Arbitrage
A strategy that produces a profit from the mispricing of an options contract compared to a synthetic option.

Conversion Factor
A factor used to calculate how many deliverable bonds are the equivalent to one notional bond in a bond future.

Convertible Bond
A bond that can be converted into ordinary shares under specific conditions.

Convertibility Clause
A clause in a contract which allows for repayment of a bond in local currency (instead of hard currency) in the event of conversion suspension. These bonds are usually issued by borrowers in emerging market countries.

Convexity
The second derivative of a financial instrument's value with respect to its yield. It is used along with duration to adjust the price of an instrument following large changes in yield.

Corner
A bear squeeze in the commodity markets. A corner occurs when a cartel of traders hold a dominant position in the physical assets underlying the futures contract. Those with a short position in the commodity will then have to pay high prices to obtain the commodity from the cartel in order to make delivery.

Correction
A sharp price movement against the prevailing trend of the market. Also know as retracement.

Corridor
The purchase of an interest rate Cap and the sale of a similar Cap which is further out-of-the-money to another party. This Caps payments due on a borrowing and reduces the cost of the hedge in return for limiting the upside.

Corridor Note
*See **accrual note**.*

Corridor Option
An option composed of a sequence of binary options which pay a fixed income for each period that the market is between two preset levels.

Cost-of-Carry
The financing charge for funds borrowed in order to buy physical stocks, index futures or equities.

Costless Collar
A collar where the income received from the sale of the short call option exactly matches the costs of purchasing the long put option.

Counterparty Risk
A risk to one party in a contract that the other party (counterparty) will fail to fulfil their obligations in full (default on the transaction). Most counterparty risk is a credit risk where the counterparty may find itself in financial difficulties. However counterparty risk also covers default risk which can include technical issues that delay the settlement of contracts such as errors in interpretation of ownership and custody.

Covariance
A statistical measure of the way in which two variables interact.

Covered Option
When the writer of an option has sufficient underlying assets or cash to cover their obligations if the option is exercised.

Covered Warrants
Warrants issued by a third party who hold enough shares, warrants or convertables in a company to cover their obligations if the warrants are exercised. Covered warrants are non-diluting, unlike conventional warrants in that they are written by third parties and the shares, warrants or convertables are already in existence.

Cox-Ross-Rubenstein Technique
A binomial technique published in 1979 by Cox, Ross and Rubenstein to assess the risk that an option will be exercised at some time in the future. It is used in the pricing of American options and takes into account market volatility.

Credit Default Swap
A Swap where one party pays a fee for protection from default by a counterparty. In return they receive a floating

payment which depends on the performance of a third party's reference security.

Credit Derivatives
Products where the returns are dependent on a set of risk factors that are related to credit quality or rating.

Credit Risk
See **counterparty risk**.

Cross-Currency Swap
The exchange of loan payments in two different currencies. The loans involved may be both fixed rate, both floating rate or one of each. Unlike straight interest rates Swaps, principal payments are usually exchanged. The Swap may involve an exchange of gross payments, but may equally only require a net payment by the party with the larger obligation. Both the sums exchanged at the start and maturity of the Swap are calculated using the same exchange rate.

Cross-Default Clause
A clause in Swap agreements which states that default by any of the counterparties (involved in the agreement) on any of its borrowings (of any type) will be deemed a default for the purposes of the Swap agreement.

Crossed Market
A peculiar situation in a market when the bid is greater than the ask. This arbitrage opportunity may occur when one market-maker sets its prices without referring to other market-makers in the same stock: Market-maker A setting its bid price higher than Market-maker B's asking price.

Cum-Warrant
A bond and warrant package traded together.

Currency Basket Options
A derivative designed to hedge multi-currency risk with a single instrument. A basket of currencies is tailored for the exact requirements of the buyer in terms of the currencies to be included and their respective amounts. They are used as an alternative to a portfolio of separate currency options for the hedging of currency risk.

Currency Exposure Method (CEM)
A method used for calculating credit risk under a Swap. The calculation includes a factor for future credit exposure and for replacement cost of the Swap.

Currency Future
The holder of a currency future may take delivery of a specific amount of a currency in exchange for a specific amount of a different currency on a specific date.

Currency Option
Gives the buyer the right, but not the obligation, to exchange a specific amount of currency for another currency on or before a specific date at a specified exchange rate.

Currency Warrant
The holder has the right to exercise a warrant into a pre-specified amount of another currency at a specific exchange rate. Currency warrants are essentially long-term currency options.

Cylinder
The purchase of a series of currency put options at the same strike price but with different maturities, and the simultaneous writing of a series of currency call options (with the same maturities) at a strike price lower than that of the put options.

D

DA
Discretionary Account

DAX
Deutsche Aktienindx (German Stock Index)

DCS
Direct Credit Substitute

DIE
Designated Investment Exchange

DO
Digital Option

DSR
Delivery Status Report

DTB
Deutsche Terminborse (now Eurex Deutschland)

DVP
Delivery Versus Payment

Day Count
The number of days used in the calculation of interest payable. Interest due is calculated by taking the applicable interest rate and multiplying it by the number of days that have elapsed and dividing by the day count. In the USA the day count is 360 for the year whilst in the UK it is 365. The most commonly used day count in Swaps is that of 30/360 which creates 12 equal length months in a year.

Day Order
An order that is cancelled if it cannot be executed during the day's trading.

Day Traders
Commodity traders who take positions and then liquidate them before the end of the trading day.

Dealer Option
A put or call on a physical commodity written by a company which deals directly in the underlying cash commodity.

Debt Warrant
A fixed rate bond with a warrant attached to it. The warrant gives the purchaser the right to buy more bonds with a (usually) lower coupon than the original bond.

Deck
All the unexecuted orders held by a floor broker.

Decompounded Rate
A scale-down rate used for a stub in a Swap. Normally only used in the US dollar market.

Default
The failure to perform on a futures contract as required by the exchange rules. This could include a failure to make a margin call as well as failure to make or take delivery.

Deferred Premium Option
An option on which the premium or part of the premium is paid at expiry. The writer of the option is exposed to the credit risk of the option buyer and so will ask a higher price than for a conventional option.

Definitive Note
A certificate representing an obligation that can be physically delivered.

Degree-Day Swaps
A Swap that pays a floating coupon which is proportional to the change in degree-days over a specified period in return for a fixed payment. The US Energy Information Administration publishes an index of degree-days which is an aggregate of 65° Fahrenheit. So, a day when the average temperature is 85° Fahrenheit will see an increase of 20° days, and one on which the average temperature is 60° Fahrenheit will see a decrease of 5° days for that day. Such Swaps are used to hedge the costs of heating in a number of industries.

Delayed Strike
A normal option once a strike price has been set. Typically set as an at-the-money option after a certain period (say, one month).

Deliverable Bond
A bond which is listed by an exchange as being acceptable in settlement of a bond future. Usually a number of bonds will be listed against any one bond future and the settler will choose the cheapest-to-deliver.

Delivery
The production (perhaps, physically) of the commodity underlying a futures contract. Most futures contracts are closed before delivery.

Delivery Month
A calendar month during which a futures contract becomes deliverable.

Delivery Point
The location at which the underlying commodity in a futures contract must be delivered.

Delivery Risk
The same as settlement risk.

Delta
The first of the factors used to describe the financial risk of derivative instruments. It is a measure of the rate of change in the value of the underlying financial instrument. And since it is the change in the underlying instrument that is the primary source of risk to any portfolio containing options it is considered the most important of The Greeks. Mathematically it can be described as:

$$Delta = \Delta = \Delta P/ \Delta U$$

Where ΔP is the change in option or portfolio value, and ΔU is the change in value of the underlying instrument.

Delta Neutrality
A strategy that this used to create a hedged portfolio that is not dependent on the movement in the price of underlying assets. Since the delta is a measure of the change in the price of an option for a given change in the price of an underlying financial instrument, a portfolio with a delta of zero will be independent of the underlying assets.

Derivative Product
A financial product, security or transaction, that derives its own value from the value of an underlying asset. This derivation of price may be direct or indirect.

Diagonal Spread
The purchase of one option and the sale of another in which both the strike and expiry are different.

Differential Swap
See cross-currency Swaps.

Digital Option
An option with a return function that has two levels. Usually one of these two levels will be zero so the holder receives the other level on expiry of the contract if it is in-the-money.

Dilution
The issuing of more shares in a company without an increase in the value of the company.

Discontinuous Barriers
A barrier option has a discontinuous barrier if there is a gap in the market. Since virtually all markets close for the weekend and any number of events could occur between Friday and Monday which alter the value of barrier options, so most barrier options may be said to have a "discontinuous barrier".

Discontinuous Lookbacks/Lookforwards
Lookback (Lookforward) options that are based on periodic samples such as daily price fixings.

Discos
Discount Bonds. Bonds issued at a discount in exchange for debt. The risk attached to an asset can be thought of (according to Markowitz) has consisting of two components: diversifiable risk, which can be made to disappear through careful combination with other assets, and non-diversifiable risk which will always have to be

borne by an investor.

Discount Currency

The currency which has a lower interest rate attached to it in a foreign exchange Swap.

Discovery

The term given to a process which gives one party the right to obtain information or documentation relating to a dispute from the counterparty in the dispute

Double Barrier Options

An option that has two barriers; one below the current spot market and one above. When either barrier is reached the appropriate action is triggered: activation for knock-ins or deactivation for knock-outs.

Barrier options of the knock-in variety must hit a barrier in order to be able to be exercised on the expiry date. Barrier options of the knock-out variety lapse upon reaching the barrier and may not be exercised at all. If the barrier is ever reached they are the equivalent (at expiry) to a European Option with the same parameters (type, strike and size).

Down and Out Option

A knock-out barrier option which lapses when the barrier is breached in a downwards direction.

Drop In Option

The opposite of a down and out option. Such options come into existence when the underlying financial instrument reaches a pre-specified level.

Dual Currency Bond

A form of bond with embedded option where the principal is repaid in dollars but the coupon is paid in a denominated currency. The interest rates received are usually higher than the existing interest rates in the denominated currency. An alternative exists, sometimes called a reverse-dual currency bond, where the principal is repaid in a specified currency but the coupon is paid in dollars.

Dual Currency Option
An option consisting of two standard currency options (with a common base) of which only one is exercisable at a expiry.

Duration
1. A measure of the sensitivity of the value of a financial instrument to a change in its yield to maturity.
2. The average maturity of all payments on a financial instrument (e.g. principal and coupon) weighted according to the discounted value of those payments.

Dynamic Hedging
The continual rebalancing of a portfolio to maintain delta neutrality. This will involve the shifting of funds between risky and risk-free investments in response to the changes in the price of the risky asset.

E

ECHO
Exchange Clearing House

ED
Eurex Deutschland

EDS
Enter Day Stop Order

EDSP
Exchange Delivery Settlement Price

EFP
Exchange For Physicals

EFS
Exchange of Futures for Swaps

EGARCH
An Exponential Garch model

EOE
European Options Exchange

EOS
Enter Stop Order

ERA
Exchange Rate Agreement

ETO
Exchange Traded Option

Edge

The difference between the price charged for an option by the writer and the theoretical price calculated using a valuation model such as the Black-Scholes formula.

Efficient Frontier

A frontier in risk-return space which produces an optimal set of portfolios. The region to the left of the frontier is unobtainable and no portfolio can be constructed which can give returns in this region. For every point to the right of the frontier, however, there is at least one portfolio that can be made from all possible investments that has an expected return and risk corresponding to that point. Typically the portfolio that lies on the Efficient Frontier will be the one which is most highly diversified.

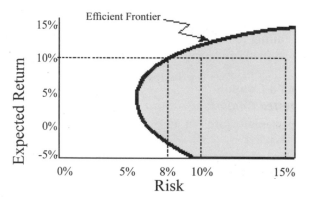

Efficient Markets Hypothesis

The theory that all stocks in an equity market reflect everything that is known about that security. In its raw form it assumes that everything that is foreseeable and every condition that can affect the supply and demand in the future (including insider information) is instantaneously reflected in the price.

Elasticity
A description of the interaction between the supply, demand, and price of a commodity. A commodity is inelastic if its supply or demand is relatively unaffected by changes in price.

Eligible Margin
Negotiable securities allowed by an exchange for the payment of margins instead of cash.

Embedded Option
Bonds that pay a fixed coupon but whose redemption values are linked to the performance of a nominated stock, index or commodity. *See also **Dual Currency Bond***.

Endowment Warrant
The call option on shares where the strike price grows at the prevailing rate of interest but also decreases in line with dividends paid by the underlying shares.

Enhanced Coupon
*See **Boosted Coupon***.

Equity Kicker
A term used to describe the issuing of warrants by a corporation alongside a bond issue as a way to encourage investors to buy the issue.

Equity Linked CD
A tradable bank loan (Certificate of Deposit) with a redemption value linked to an underlying equity.

Equity-Linked Foreign Exchange Contract
A currency Option whose face amount is linked to the value of a foreign asset.

Equity Option
A contract that gives the holder the right but not the obligation to buy or sell specified equities at a specific price on or before a specified date.

Equity Swap
A two party agreement where one counterparty pays an equity (equity index) return in exchange for a fixed or floating money market return. For example one party pays a six-month Libor and receives from the counterparty the FTSE plus associated dividends.

Equity Warrant
An optional instrument that may be attached to a (usually) fixed rate bond. It is a effectively a call option on the underlying equity of the issuing company. Unlike an option, however, when a warranty is exercised the holder receives shares from the issuing company. An option, on the other hand, gives the owner the right to buy shares from any party that already holds the underlying equity. Warrants, therefore, usually dilute the holdings of existing shareholders (as opposed to options which do not). Warrants may be issued either in American style or European style and the holder is not entitled to dividends until the warrants are exercised into the underlying equity.

Euro Bond
A long-term bearable bond issued by a company or government outside its country of origin and sold to buyers who pay for it in a Euro currency.

Euro Dollar
US dollars deposited in a bank outside the USA and used for trade within Europe. Similarly Euro Yen.

European-style Option
An option that may only be exercised on its expiry date. This is in contrast to an American option which may be exercised at any time up to and including the expiry date. Therefore it has the disadvantage that the holder is unable to benefit from favourable price movements of the underlying equity during the options lifetime.

Exact Replicating Portfolio
A portfolio that follows a specified index or basket of financial instruments without error. A continuously re-balanced delta hedge is considered sufficient to create an exact replicating portfolio.

Excess Return
The difference between the return on a portfolio and the return that could have been realised by investment of the same amount of funds in a risk-free investment.

Exchange Risk
The risk that movement in exchange rates between an investor's home currency and the currency in which he may hold financial investments moves against him. This risk can wipe out any profits made by overseas investments and can turn a profitable situation into a loss. Exchange risk is one of the main risks that are hedged through the use of futures, forwards, options, and Swaps.

Exchange Traded Contracts
Financial contracts that are traded on an exchange and subject to the exchange's regulations and specifications. As opposed to over-the-counter (OTC) transactions which are opaque in nature and whose details are fixed by the parties involved.

Execution Risk
The risk that an error will occur during the execution of a trade or series of trades.

Exercise Price
The price that an equity warrant holder or options holder will need to pay for each unit of the underlying financial instrument. The term "exercise price" usually refers to warrants whereas "strike price" refers to options; however the terms are often confused and have become virtually interchangeable.

Exotic Options
An option offering a variation from the standard European or American call and put options. Exotic options are the fastest growing area in the derivatives business.

Expiry Date
The day on which a European style option (or warrant) may be exercised. It is also the last day on which an American style option (or warrant) may be exercised.

Exploding Options
Reverse knock-out barrier options with the rebate equal to the intrinsic value at the barrier. Similar to a vertical spread of European options but locks in (or pays immediately) the maximum profit if the barrier is reached.

Exposure
The total amount of risk run by an investor. Often used to refer to quantity of money that an investor stands to loose if their investments collapse.

Extrinsic Value
The component of an options value which comes about purely by virtue of the time remaining before the expiry

date. Whatever the states of the market there is always a chance that an option position will move into profit (or further into profit) and the extrinsic value, or time value, is a monetary assessment of this chance.

Ex-Warrant
A bond or other financial instrument that was originally issued with warrants attached but whose warrants have now been exercised or traded to another party.

F

FAS
Free Alongside Ship

FAST
Fast Automated Screen Trading

FAZ
Frankfurter Allgemeine Zeitung

FIBOR
Frankfurt Interbank Offered Rate

FIONA
Frankfurt Interbank Over Night Average

FOB
Free on Board

FOFs
Futures and Options Funds

FOK
Fill or Kill Order

FOR
Free on Rail

FRA
Forward Rate Agreement

FRN
Floating Rate Note

FRS
Financial Reporting Standards

FSA
Forward Spread Agreement (also Financial Services Act)

FTA
Financiele Termijnmarket Amsterdam

FX
Foreign Exchange

FXA
Foreign Exchange Agreement

Face Value
The Value that appears on the face of a bond as opposed to its market value.

Fair Value
Generally accepted to be when an option or warrant is priced at the same level as a result of an options pricing model. If the price is higher than that calculated by the model then it is considered "expensive", and if it is less than calculated by the model it is considered "cheap".

Fairway Bond
Another name for bonds or notes such as accrual notes or corridor notes which accrue interest if the index stays within a certain range.

Fibonacci Numbers
A sequence of numbers where the next number in the sequence is always equal to the sum of the previous two numbers. It is at the mathematical basis of the Elliott Wave Theory used to predict market movements.

Financial Future
A futures contract where the underlying asset is not a physical commodity, such as currency futures and interest rate futures.

Financial Risk
The chance of exposure to a monetary loss.

First Notice Day
The first day that sellers can present a notice of intention to deliver a commodity against a futures contract through the Exchange Clearing House.

Fixed-Fixed Swap
A circus Swap where both streams of payments are at a fixed rate.

Fixed-Floating Swap
See Circus Swap.

Fixed Income
A bond (or other security) that pays a guaranteed rate of interest on specified dates in the future.

Flex Option
An exchange traded option that does not have the standard terms of options listed on that exchange. One or more of the details such as strike price and expiry date are determined between the market-maker and the customer.

Floating-Floating Swap
See Basis Swap.

Floating Rate Note
An interest bearing security with options to alter the coupon it pays on specified dates in the future.

Floor
An over-the-counter financial instrument which is the equivalent to buying a series of interest rate put options with different expiry dates but at the same strike price. Used by lenders to ensure a set minimum interest rate.

Floor Broker
An agent who executes orders on the floor of an exchange. Floor brokers are not usually allowed to trade on their own account.

Floor Traders
Members of an exchange who execute orders on the trading floor of an exchange for themselves as well as their customers. Also known as "locals" and "scalpers".

Floortion
An option on a Floor.

Foreign Exchange Future (Option)
*See **Currency Future (Option)**.*

Foreign Exchange Swap
An over-the-counter financial instrument where two parties exchange an amount of one currency for an amount of another currency for a specified period. No coupon payments are made in either direction during the Swap period. However the exchange rate that is used when the Swap matures is calculated from the difference between the interest rates applicable to the two currencies at the beginning of the Swap.

Forwardation
See **Contango**.

Forward Contract
A contract to buy or sell an underlying financial instrument for a fixed price at a specific (delivery) date sometime in the future. The forward price is determined by the spot price plus the "cost-of-carry". The cost-of-carry itself increases in proportion to the rate of interest and storage charges and decreases as a function of income from the underlying financial instrument (such as dividends and interest).

Forward Conversion
An arbitrage opportunity that occurs in the currency option market when options and forwards become mispriced relative to one another. The usual strategy that results in an arbitrage profit involves the purchase of a currency forward and the simultaneous writing of a call and the purchase of a put option.

Forward-Forward
An agreement between two parties for the purchase (sale) of an underlying financial instrument in the future which is agreed with a delayed starting date.

Forward Forward Curve
The forward curve on a specific date in the future (based on the current Forward Curve).

Forward Rate Agreement
The contract in which one party receives a fixed interest rate whilst paying a floating rate and the other party receives the floating rate while paying the fixed rate. An interest rate is agreed between the parties for a (notional) principal sum over a specified period in the future. On the

settlement date (start of the specified period) the seller of the FRA will pay the buyer the difference between the agreed rate of interest and the prevailing rate if actual interest rates (for the forward period) are higher than the agreed rate. If, on the other hand, actual interest rates are lower then the buyer will pay the seller.

Forward Reversal
The opposite to a forward conversion. It involves a simultaneous sale of a currency forward, purchase of a call and writing of a put in order to realise a risk-free profit on the currency options market.

Forward Swap
Contracts which start on a specified date at some time in the future instead of the day on which the contract was made.

Free on Board
Indicates that the price of a commodity includes all the costs associated with delivery, inspection and other loading costs involved in putting that commodity on a carrier such as a ship or train.

Free Supply
Stocks of a commodity that are available from commercial bodies as opposed to the Government.

Front-End Load
A financial instrument is front-loaded when a sales charge or commission is paid for the investment at the time of purchase.

Front End Payment
A single payment made at the beginning of a new contract.

Fundamental Analysis
An analysis of the market that examines underlying factors which affect the supply and demand of a financial instrument.

Fungible
A financial instrument that can be exchanged for another of the same type.

Future
A standardised contract to buy or sell (take delivery or make delivery) of a specified quantity or a grade of a commodity (physical or financial) at a specified price on a fixed date in the future. Futures contracts, unlike forward contracts contain standardised terms which allow them to be traded on recognised exchanges.

Futures Option
An option listed on an exchange that settles into a futures contract.

Futures Roll
The buying or selling of one-month's futures contracts in favour of the next period's futures contracts. Refers to rolling out the futures to longer maturitys.

Futures Strip
A series of short-term futures contracts which will generate a return for a period equal to the length of the strip when grossed up.

G-10
The 10 leading world industrial nations

GD
Good-for-the-Day Order

GEMM
Gilt-Edged Market-maker

GFOF
Geared Futures and Options Fund

GLOBX
Global Electronic Exchange

GTC
Good-Till-Cancelled Order

Gamma
A measure of a rate at which an options delta is changing. If the sensitivity of the value of an option to changing values of the underlying instrument were linear then only delta would be needed to described its movements. However it is not a straight line so gamma needs to be used as a second-order coefficient which gives an indication as to the curvature of the option value/underlying value curve.

The curve will have the mathematical description:

$$(\Gamma/2)U^2 + \Delta U + C$$

Where Γ is Gamma, ΔU is the change in the value of the underlying instrument and C is a constant.

A positive gamma depicts a curve which opens upwards, whilst a negative gamma depicts one which opens downwards. In practice gamma, is a measure of how close an option is to expiry and how close a price of the underlying financial instrument is to the strike price.

Gap

A gap is created when a financial instrument trades in a range which is entirely above or below the previous days range. On a chart of prices versus time there will be a "gap" between one days high and the next days low.

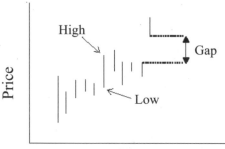

GARCH

Generalised Autoregressive Conditional Heteroskedasticity. A complex volatility forecasting model used when tranquil periods are interspersed with bursts of high volatility.

Garman-Kohalhagen Model

An adaptation of the Black-Scholes model to fit currency options by adding another variable to take into account the interest rate of a second currency.

Gearing

1. A ratio of borrowings to capital.
2. The ratio of the price of an underlying equity to the warrant price per share.

Generic Swap
Also known as a "plain vanilla" Swap, usually involves the exchange of a strip of fixed rate payments for a strip of floating rate payments (or vice versa) with a counterparty.

Ghost Feature
The correction on a moving average curve seen at the end of a period when a major event, such as a sharp market fall or rise, drops out of the moving average calculation.

Gilt Strip
A zero coupon bond that is either a coupon or the principal of a UK Government bond (trading separately).

Good Till Cancelled
An order given to a broker which remains in place until executed or the customer cancels it (as opposed to a day order).

Grantor
*See **Writer**.*

Greeks
A set of factors, written as Greek symbols in algebraic equations, which are used to model the behaviour of options in relation to changes in the value of the underlying financial instruments, volatility, interest rates, and time. *See **Delta**, **Gamma**, **Vega**, **Rho** and **Theta**.*

Guaranteed Fund
A synthetic equity portfolio which offers a guaranteed minimum return (equal to the coupon on the bond divided by the total sum invested). The synthetic portfolio is created by purchasing an index call option and deep-discount security.

H

HH
Heavy Hitter

HIBID
Hongkong Interbank Bid Rate

HIBOR
Hongkong Interbank Offered Rate

HKFE
Hongkong Futures Exchange

HSI
Hang Sen Index

Haircut
The excess of a financial instruments market value over and above the loan for which it is serving as capital.

Hamster Option
A proprietary instrument which receives and keeps a fixed coupon for every day the underlying financial instrument stays within a specified range.

Harmless Warrant
A warrant that is issued with and may be detached from a callable bond. Prior to the call date the bond must be surrendered before the warrant can be exercised.

Heavy Hitter
An individual, group of individuals, institution, or company with substantial funds available for investing in the derivatives market.

Hedging
The protection of an investment against possible loss by buying investments of a fixed price for future delivery.

Hedging Risk
The risk that a transaction is not hedged properly. This could be because the correct financial instruments are not available to create a perfect hedge, through mis-calculation, or by incorrect execution in the market.

Hermaphrodite Option
Another name for an AC/DC option where the purchaser can choose for it to be either a call option or a put option.

Heteroskedasticity
Volatility which is not constant.

Historical Volatility
An estimate of the "riskiness" of a portfolio based on actual market value fluctuations.

Homoskedasticity
Volatility which is constant.

Host Bond
A bond on which warrants are attached.

Hurricane Bond
A catastrophe bond which pays a coupon that decreases if a hurricane occurs.

I

ICC
Intermarket Clearing Corporation

ICCH
International Commodities Clearing House

IDB
Intermediary Dealer Broker

IMI
International Market Index

IMM
International Money Market

IO
Interest Only

IOC
Immediate or Cancel Order

IOM
Index and Options Market

IPE
International Petroleum Exchange

IRG
Interest Rate Guarantee

ISDA
International Swap Dealers Association

ISE
International Stock Exchange

ISMA
International Securities Market Association

ITM
In-The-Money

Implied Repo Rate
The return on a cash-and-carry arbitrage of buying a bond then selling a futures contract and delivering the bond. The cheapest-to-deliver bond (in a futures contract) will be the bond with the highest implied repo rate.

Implied Volatility
The implied volatility of a portfolio is a measure of the "riskiness" of the portfolio as it is now as opposed to some period in the past (*see **historical volatility***). Estimates of implied volatility are made from option prices being used to back calculate the volatility in models such as the Black-Scholes model.

In-The-Money Option
An option is in-the-money if it has an intrinsic value. A call is in-the-money if its strike price is below the current price of the underlying financial instrument. A put is in-the-money if its strike price is above the current price of the underlying financial instrument.

Index Amortising Swap
A Swap whose notional amount declines in each specified period by an amount that depends on the level of interest rates.

Index Future

A financial instrument that gives the purchaser a standard basket of stocks (those which are used to calculate the index) on the delivery date.

Index Option

An option on index futures.

Inflation Linked Bonds

Bonds with coupons that depend on the rate of inflation or an inflation related index.

Initial Margin

A deposit required by an exchange at the time a futures position is established or an option is sold in order to assure the customer meets their obligations.

Instalment Options

Options where a sequence of payments must be made before the owner receives the right to exercise the option at expiry. The owner may choose to abandon the option at any point by ceasing the payment of instalments.

Instrument

A general term used to cover all types of securities.

Interest Rate Future

The buyer of an interest rate future acquires the right to receive a money market deposit or coupon-bearing instrument on a specific date in the future.

Interest Rate Guarantees

Options on forward rate agreements.

Interest Rate Option
1. The owner of an interest rate option has the right, but not the obligation, to receive (in the case of a put option) or pay (call option) a specific rate of interest or a specified notional principal over a specified period.
2. Options on interest rate futures and forward rate agreements.

Interest Rate Swap
A stream of payments calculated on one basis (fixed or floating) on a notional principal exchanged with a counterparty for a stream of payments calculated on the other basis and in the same currency. Unlike cross-currency Swaps they involve no physical exchange of the principal. They are used by all manner of investors to transform their income streams from fixed to floating and vice versa.

Intermediary
A financial institution that puts two Swap counterparties together for a fee.

Intrinsic Value
The difference between the strike price and the market value of the underlying financial instrument plus (or minus) the cost-of-carry. For European options the intrinsic value is the difference between the strike price and the current forward price for the underlying financial instrument at the expiry date. But for an American option the intrinsic value is the difference between the strike price and the current Swap price.

Inverse Floater
A floating rate note that receives a coupon which decreases when the underlying index rate increases.

Inverted Market
A futures market in which the closer months are selling at a premium to the more distant months. Usually it refers to a market where current supplies are relatively scarce but where new supplies are expected soon. For example the wheat market may become inverted a few months before a bumper harvest is expected.

Invisible Supply
Uncounted stocks of a commodity in the hands of wholesalers, manufacturers and producers. This supply cannot be identified accurately and are "outside" normal commercial channels but theoretically available for the market.

Iron Butterfly
The purchase of an out-of-the-money put, an at-the-money put, an at-the-money call and an out-of-the-money call.

JEC
Joint Exchanges Committee

JGB
Japanese Government Bond

JSDA
Japanese Securities Dealers Association

Jamming
Executing a large sell or buy order in stages by going to the first market-maker with a small order and hitting the bid or offer price and then repeating the process with a sequence of other market-makers. The process has the aim of driving the price lower or higher for another purpose.

Jelly Roll
A synthetic futures roll using options.

Junk Bonds
Slang for a high risk security that receives low ratings and can then produce high yield so long as it docsn't go into default.

K

KLOFFE
Kuala Lumpa Options and Financial Futures Exchange

KSE
Korea Stock Exchange

Kappa
*See **Vega***.

Kerb Trading
Unofficial trading between members of an exchange outside designated trading hours.

Knock-In Option
An option which kicks-in when a price crosses a particular barrier.

Knock-Out Option
An option that "dies" when a price crosses a particular barrier.

LCE
London Commodity Exchange

LCH
London Clearing House

LDB
Liquidity Data Bank

LEAPS
Long-Term Equity AnticiPation Securities

LIBID
London Interbank Bid or Deposit Rate

LIBOR
London Interbank offered Rate

LIFFE
London International Financial Futures and Options Exchange

LIMEAN
The mean of LIBID and LIBOR

LIPS
LIBOR Indexed Principal Swaps

LME
London Metal Exchange

LOCH
London Options Clearing House

LSE
London Stock Exchange

Ladder Option
An option similar to a look-back option but where the most favourable price is quantified. Upon expiry the pay off is determined according to which of the "rungs" were achieved during the lifetime of the contract. If the underlying asset reached a price which falls between two rungs then the lower rung is used for the pay off for ladder call options and the higher rung for ladder put options.

Ladder Periodic Cap
A periodic Cap that behaves similar to a ladder option. The pay off is dependent upon the highest or lowest rung of the ladder that LIBOR reached during the period specified in the Cap. The rung levels of the ladder usually change from one period to the next.

Last Trading Day
The day on which trading stops for the maturing delivery month.

Legal Risk
1. The risk that a loss may be incurred as a result of an error or omission of legal documents or procedures followed in the course of a transaction.
2. The risk that legislation may not be adequate to cover all of the possible default events in a very complex derivative transaction.

Legging

The sale of one leg of a spread (straddle or strangle) following a sharp movement in the relevant underlying financial instruments value. This is a risky procedure since the market may bounce back and the leggor may be forced to buy the leg of the spread back again. At the end of the day the portfolio will be unchanged but two lots of transaction costs will have been incurred (known as whipsawing).

Leverage

The use of derivatives to generate a market exposure greater than would be achieved by purchasing the underlying financial instrument. Small movements in the market therefore produce greater gains or losses than for a non-levered position. The greater the leverage the larger the profit and loss swings per unit change in the underlying financial instrument.

Liability Swap

A Swap which is combined with a bond in order to change the structure of the bond. The bond and the Swap may or may not have been issued together.

LIBOR-In-Arrears Swap

A Swap in which the Libor value is fixed two days before the payment date.

LIBOR Indexed Principal Swap

An amortising Swap which depends on the change in LIBOR.

Life of Contract
The time between the beginning of trading in a particular futures contract and the last day of trading in the delivery month.

Limit Buying Order
An order placed in the market which instructs a broker to buy (or sell) any form of contract if a specific (target) price is touched. If the specified price is reached the broker must still endeavour to complete the transaction on the best possible terms rather than just accept the target price.

Limit Move
A change in price of a financial instrument that has moved by the "price limit" during one trading session.

Limit Order
An order where the buyer has set a limit on the price or the time allowed for the contract to be completed.

Liquid Market
A market where there are plenty of opportunities to sell or buy a financial instrument.

Liquidation
The sale or purchase of futures contracts to close a position.

Liquidity Risk
1. The risk that there will be no market for a financial asset or a contract at the time a holder wishes to buy, sell or exercise. Forward rate agreements, for example, cannot be traded in the open market and a position can only be offset by making one or more separate transactions in the

other direction. Similarly over-the-counter options are difficult to trade since they are designed for individual requirements. So, both FRA's and OTC options carry a high liquidity risk.

2. The risk that a counterparty in a transaction will default on their obligations owing to cash flow or solvency problems.

Listed Option
A standardised option contract traded on a recognised exchange.

Live Price
The price given to a buyer or seller which is only valid during the time it takes the buyer or seller to respond to the offer.

Local
See Floor Trader.

Locked Market
A very unusual condition in the market where the bid equals the ask. Since a locked market can only occur with two or more market-makers the opportunity for arbitrage using the other bids and asks usually unlocks the market pretty quickly.

London International Financial Futures and Options Exchange (LIFFE)
Was formed by a merger of the London Traded Options Market and the London International Financial Futures Exchange in March 1992.

Long

An investor is "long" if they have bought a financial instrument. The opposite of going short.

Long-Term Equity AnticiPation Securities

Normal call and put options with expiry dates greater than nine months.

Look-Back Option

An option that can be exercised at the best price achieved during its lifetime.

Look-Back Period Cap

A periodic Cap with where the pay-off is determined by the highest or lowest level that Libor Caps reached during the period of the Cap.

MAS
Monetary Authority of Singapore

MATIF
Marché à Terme des Instruments Financiers

MBS
Mortgage Backed Security

MEFF
Derivatives Exchange in Spain

MIF
Derivatives Exchange in Italy

MINE
Market Indexed Notes

MITI
Ministry for International Trade and Industry (Japan)

MIT
Market If Touched Order

MKT
Market Order

MMI
Major Market Index (US)

MOC
Market on Close Order

MOF
Ministry of Finance

MONEP
Marché Des Options Negotiables De Paris

MQP
Mandatory Quote Period

Macaulay Duration
The modified duration multiplied by $(1 + Y/N)$ where N is the number of coupon payments each year and Y is the yield. It provides a weighted average of time until a particular financial instrument pays its cash flows.

Maintenance Margin
An amount of money that must be maintained in the margin account while a futures position remains open. If the deposit drops below the maintenance margin level a margin call will be made.

Margin
1. The Clearing House on a derivatives exchange acts as in intermediary in every transaction and is effectively a counterparty in every single trade. It therefore incurs default risk in that the other party may fail to meet its obligations. To counterbalance this it requires some form of insurance via the deposit of a sum of money (initial margin) with the exchange.

   Every traders position is marked to "market" on a daily basis to assess overall exposure. If the markets have gone against a particular trader and their position is worse than on a previous day's close, the trader's margin account will be debited by an amount to cover their potential loss. If, on the other hand, their position is better than on a previous day's close then the margin account will be credited.

Should a trader's position continually be worse than the previous day and the amounts debited from their margin account be greater than the initial margin placed with the exchange then a "margin call" will be made, requiring the trader to make a further deposit. A similar call may be made by the exchange if market volatility increases to such an extent that they believe potential losses may be greater than the margin account.

Some exchanges will accept collateral in addition to or as well as cash to cover margin payments.

2. The amount of money left from a transaction once costs have been covered.

Margrabe Option
The option to exchange one asset for another, such as a cross currency option.

Market-if-Touched
An order to buy or sell a derivatives contract which becomes a market order if a specific price is reached (in the relevant direction).

Market Order
An order to buy or sell a contract for immediate execution.

Market Risk
The risk associated with the field in which a company acts or in which a financial instrument is traded. As opposed to specific risk where a single company or financial instrument is affected, the market risk element reflects the fact that the entire market or market segment may be affected by outside events.

Marking to Market
The daily valuation of a trader's position on a particular exchange. The relevant closing prices are compared to the purchase prices of the contract for the purposes of margin credits and debits.

Market Indexed Notes
A security where the principal repayment is guaranteed and the coupon payments consist of a fixed rate element and a secondary element which depends on the performance of a recognised index.

Markowitz Model
The original portfolio theory put forward by Harry Markowitz in the 1950's. He was the first to formalise and quantify the idea of diversification and its application to financial instruments. The main points of his model were:

✔ The overall portfolio risk is less than the weighted average of the individual risks.

✔ The portfolio risk will be lower the more diversified the assets.

✔ The risk of an individual asset can be thought of consisting of two parts: one which can be diversified away and the other which will always be present.

Master Document
Usually a legal document which covers all the general terms and conditions of a contract and are agreed by both parties.

Maturity
The date when a financial instrument becomes due for payment.

Maximum/Minimum Price Fluctuation
See Limit Move.

Mause Option
A range option that pays when the market increases within a narrow, upward-sloping corridor.

Millennium Bond
A bond that matures in 1,000 years which is used primarily to reduce the requirement for refinancing.

Mismatch Swap
Swaps where the two parties involved end up with different payment profiles. One of the parties involved will therefore incur credit risk.

Mismatched Risk
The risk in a Swap portfolio when the terms of the off-setting Swaps do not match exactly (for example a mismatch between one and six month LIBOR).

Model Risk
The risk that a financial model used to calculate a price or value will be incorrect and a loss will occur.

Modified Duration
The first derivative of a financial instrument's value with respect to the change in its yield.

Momentum Indicator
The difference between the current market price of an instrument and the price of the same instrument a certain number of days ago plotted against time.

Money at Risk
A risk measure used to aggregate all the risky positions to which an individual, company or institution may be exposed.

Money-back Option
A knock-out option with a discount equal to the initial premium.

Monthly Income Preferred Shares
Preferred shares that pay monthly dividends, usually referred to as simply MIPS.

Mortgage Backed Security
A security that derives its cash flows and market value from bonds, loans, or notes with an interest in a piece of property.

Moving Average
A charting technique used on a sample of market data by creating an average over a number of days less than the total in the group. This technique eliminates fluctuations in the data and emphasises the direction in the trend.

Mutual Termination Option
An option containing a clause that allows either party to the agreement to unconditionally terminate the contract or parts of the contract on one or more pre-specified dates before the maturity. The master agreement for a mutual termination option will include an agreed formula for the valuation of the outstanding transactions on the specified dates.

Myf
Colloquialism for the best possible option.

NASD
National Association of Securities Dealers (USA)

NASDAQ
National Association of Securities Dealers Automated Quote System (US)

NFA
National Futures Association

NOB
Notes Over Bonds

NSE
Nagoya Stock Exchange

NYBID
New York Interbank Bid Rate

NYBOR
New York Interbank Offered Rate

NYCE
New York Cotton Exchange

NYFE
New York Futures Exchange

NYMEX
New York Mercantile Exchange

NYSE
New York Stock Exchange

NZFOE
New Zealand Futures and Options Exchange

Naked Option
The writer of an option is in a naked position if they do not have enough cash available to accept delivery of the underlying financial instrument (in the case of a put), or insufficient underlying financial instrument to be able to fulfil their obligations if the option is exercised (in the case of a call).

Naked Rebate
The purchase of a barrier option with a rebate and the sale of the same barrier option without a rebate. Sometimes called one-touch binary options.

Naked Warrant
A warrant issued without a host bond.

Nearby Delivery
The futures contract which is closest to maturity

Nearbys
The nearest delivery months of a futures market.

Negative Carry
The situation where a futures contract trades at a premium to the underlying when it nears maturity, brought about by returns to the investor (such as dividends and coupons) that out-weigh the cost-of-carry.

Net Position
The difference between the open long-contracts and open short-contracts held by individual, company or institution in a particular futures contract month.

New Asset Value
The total of assets less liabilities plus (or minus) the value of open positions marked-to-the-market divided by the number of units for a commodity pool.

New Money Bonds
Bonds issued by banks willing to lend funds to countries following debt restructuring.

Ninety/Ten Strategy
A portfolio strategy where 90% of available funds is invested in short-term risk-free instruments and the remaining 10% is used to buy options or index futures options.

No-Arbitrage Conditions
The assumption in financial models that prices are re-balanced continuously so that there is never an opportunity to make a risk-free profit.

Nominal Price
The price used in place of a closing price for a futures month when no recent trading has taken place. Usually the average of the bid and ask prices.

Non-Deliverable Forwards
A forward contract on a non-convertible foreign currency that settles into a convertible currency (usually the US Dollar).

Non-Deliverable Swaps
A cross-currency Swap where one or more of the currencies is a non-convertible foreign currency. Settlement of the non-convertible currency is made in a convertible currency (usually the US Dollar).

Non-Disclosure
The failure to disclose a material fact to a counterparty which would be required in the making of a decision regarding a financial investment.

Normalising
A statistical adjustment made to data to put it within a normal or standard range.

Notice of Delivery
*See **Delivery Notice**.*

Notional Amount
The stated amount in a derivatives contract on which payments depend.

Novation
The method by which one part of an over-the-counter agreement is exchanged for another part in such a way that all other terms and conditions stay the same.

OBO
Order Book Official (US)

OCC
Options Clearing Corporation (US)

OCO
One Cancels the Other Order

OEM
Original Exposure Method

OFT
Office of Fair Trading

OIE
Overseas Investment Exchange

OIP
Official Index Period

OIS
Overnight Indexed Swaps

OPEC
Organisation of Petroleum Exporting Countries

OSE
Osaka Securities Exchange (Japan)

OTC
Over-The-Counter

OTM
Out-Of-The-Money

Off-Balance Sheet Assets Liabilities
Derivative products such as futures, options and Swaps which do not appear on a company's balance sheet.

Off-Market Swaps
A below-market Swap contract where the fixed-rate receiver gets a rate lower than the going Swap rate. Also an above-market Swap where the fixed-rate receiver gets a rate above the going Swap rate.

Off-The-Run Treasury
An old on-the-run issue once a treasury has issued a new on-the-run issue.

Offer
The price at which a market-maker is willing to sell, as opposed to bid.

Offset
The liquidation of a long (or short) futures position through the sale or purchase of an equal number of contracts of the same delivery month.

Omega
The dividend sensitivity of an option with respect to the change in price of the underlying.

Omnibus Account
A futures account where the transactions made by two or more individuals, companies or institutions are combined instead of being designated separately.

On-The-Run Treasury
The most recently issued treasury note or bond with a given initial maturity (a current coupon issue).

One-Off Agreement
A document for a particular deal, as opposed to a master agreement for a series of deals.

One-Touch Option
See Binary Option.

One-Touch Contingent Premium Options
The purchase of a standard European option directly financed by the sale of a one-touch binary option.

One Way Coloured Note
See One way floating rate note.

One Way Floater
See One way floating rate note.

One Way Floating Rate Note
A floating rate note where the rates can only move in one direction or the other (either up or down). Also known as a one way coloured note, one way floater, sticky floater, or ratchet floater.

Open
The transactions made on an exchange at the beginning of a trading session.

Open Interest

The total number of futures contracts that are currently outstanding. This figure is used as an indicator of liquidity of the market and to whether the outlook is bullish or bearish.

Open Outcry

A decreasingly used method of trading futures and options on an exchange floor in pits.

Opening Range

The range of related prices at which transactions took place at the opening of the market.

Operational Risk

The risk of losses being made on a derivatives transaction as a result of systems failure or error in the following of procedures.

Opportunity Cost

The risk of "perceived" losses being made by way of the fact that money or other assets could have been put to better used while tied up in a particular contract.

Option

The holder of a call option has the right, but not an obligation, to buy a certain number of financial instruments at a set price on a specific day. The holder of a put option has the right to sell a certain number of financial instruments at a set price on a specific day. As before, it is a right, and not an obligation.

The number of units of a financial instrument involved depends on how many options contracts have been purchased or sold. The price at which the instrument can be bought is known as the exercise price, and taking up your option to buy or sell is known as exercising your options.

The date on which you may choose to exercise your options (or not as the case may be) is known as the expiration date of the contracts.

European options only allow for exercising of the option on a specific date. Whereas American options allow the holders the right to buy or sell on or before a specific date.

Option Pricing

The pricing of options is a relatively complex procedure involving the use of mathematical models. It is based primarily around probability theory and is, of course, a prediction of the future. The main factors that go into the pricing of options are:

✔ The option to do what?;

✔ the price of the underlying;

✔ time;

✔ interest, and

✔ volatility.

All of the factors involved seek to compensate the writer of the options for the relative amount of risk that they incur. For example, the first factor "the option to do what?" will compensate the writer more for an American style option than a European style option. This is because the latter involves less uncertainty on behalf of the seller of the option.

The price of the underlying is important as it dictates whether the option is in-the-money, out-of-the-money or at-the-money.

The time to go to the expiry date of the option has a bearing on the opportunity that an option has to move into profit or greater profit.

The interest rates need to be taken into consideration since the funds required for an options contract could be earning risk-free rates of interest in the market.

And the volatility is perhaps one of the most important factors in the various models as the greater the size of price swings around the mean the greater the cost of hedging for sellers of options.

Order Execution
The handling of an order by a broker from the receipt of the order through the exchange including the transaction itself and the return of confirmation back to the customer.

Original Exposure Method
A method used for calculating credit risk in a Swap contract. This method ignores the marked-to market value and uses the original exposure on the Swap. Compared to the current exposure method it generally has higher factors of future credit exposure.

Original Margin
See Initial Margin.

Out-Of-The-Money Option
An out-of-the-money option would yield a loss if exercised immediately. It has an intrinsic value of zero, so includes call options when the strike price is above the current market price and put options where the strike price is below the current market price.

Outperformance Option
This form of derivatives contract pays the difference between the market returns on two separate financial instruments or indices.

Outside Barrier Option
An option in which a barrier may be triggered by movement in another market "outside" the one in which the original transaction has taken place.

Overbought
A technical analysis situation where the market price is deemed to have risen too steeply considering the underlying fundamental factors.

Oversold
A technical analysis situation where the market price is deemed to have declined too far considering the underlying fundamental factors.

Over-The-Counter Options
Over-the-counter transactions are specifically created to suit both parties in a contract. In other words the contracts are not subject to any exchange's regulations and do not need to be in specific units of trading or mature on any specific day.

P&S
Purchase and Sale

PIBOR
Paris Interbank Offered Rate

PLO
Public Limit Order

PO
Principal Only

POM
Public Order Member

PPI
Producer Price Index

PRS
Price Reporting System

Pack
A forward strip.

Paper
The term used as a description for financial instruments which have been issued in order to raise cash.

Par
When the price is 100% of the principal value.

Par Yield Curve

A curve which measures yield over time.

Parallel Loan

A loan swapped between two companies in different countries. One company who can arrange a loan at preferential rates in their own country lends that amount to another company in a different country (who would not be able to arrange a similar loan at such good rates of interest). A reciprocal loan is then made in the other direction. In a true parallel loan, the values remain on the balance sheets of the two companies involved and hence both carry default risk.

Participating Forward

The buyer of a participating forward nominates the degree to which they wish to "participate" in any upside or downside, or, alternatively the forward exchange rate. The seller of the contract then sets the parameter that has not been nominated by the purchaser. The cost of the contract is then incorporated into the strike price.

Payer

The party in a Swap agreement which pays the fixed rate and receives the floating rate.

Periodic Cap

An interest rate Cap where the strikes on the Caplets are allowed to differ.

Pit Trading

Trading on the floor of an exchange by open outcry.

Plain Vanilla Swap
A basic fixed-floating interest rate Swap. *See **Generic Swap**.*

Point
The minimum fluctuation in the price of a financial instrument.

Political Risk
The element of financial risk which covers the actions of Governments. It covers the whole range of possibilities from devaluation of a currency and changing of interest rates through to the possibility of coups and the commencement of hostilities with another country.

Pooled Option
A compound option taken out by two or more individuals, corporations or institutions.

Portfolio Insurance
*See **Dynamic Hedging**.*

Portfolio Margining
The method by which a trader's margin payment is calculated by referring to the net total of all their positions instead of on a contract by contract basis.

Position
A description of a market commitment to buy or to sell. The buyer of a futures contract has taken a long position and the seller of a futures contract has taken a short position.

Position-Delta

A weighted sum of all the deltas associated with derivatives in a portfolio. A portfolio which is delta-neutral should be "protected" against small movements in the value of underlying securities.

Position Limit

The maximum number of futures contracts that can be held by an individual, corporation or institution in regulated commodities.

Position Trader

A trader who buys or sells contracts and holds them for an extended period, as opposed to a day trader.

Position Trading

Trades that are based on the expectation of where prices are going but are entirely consistent with the accepted market level of volatility.

Positive Carry

The situation when the return on a financial instrument exceeds the funding cost for the instrument. For example a futures contract trading at a discount to the underlying financial instrument when it is very close to maturity.

Preferred Share

Receives a fixed dividend and has preference over common stock in the case of bankruptcy or liquidation.

Premium

*See **Option Pricing***. It is the amount paid by the buyer of an option to the writer of the option in compensation for the risk that the writer will incur.

Premium Currency
The currency with the higher interest rate in a foreign exchange Swap.

Premium Swap
A Swap where the fixed rate is above the market rate, and hence a premium must be paid to the floating rate receiver.

Prepayment Risk
The risk that an underlying security (for example a mortgage backed security) will be pre-paid in order to refinance a position. The risk is that the pre-payment may occur at a time when it is difficult to find an investment that will generate similar returns to the original security.

Price Limit
1. The maximum movement in the value of a financial instrument allowed in one day on a particular exchange.
2. The maximum price at which a contract may be executed.

Principal
A large institution that has a seat on an exchange and are allowed to trade for their own account, as opposed to brokers.

Principal Only
A security which receives only the principal repayments from an underlying mortgage-backed security.

Principal Only Swap
A Swap where a specified amount in two different currencies is exchanged but no interest payments are made.

Instead the sum outstanding in either direction is altered at regular intervals during the life of the Swap.

Purchase and Sale Statement
A printed statement sent by a broker to a customer when a derivatives position has been liquidated or offset.

Put-Call Parity
When the value of a call option less the value of a put option is equal to the underlying futures price less the strike price for the two options.

Put Option
The right, but not an obligation, to sell an underlying asset at a predetermined price on or before a specific date.

Put Ratio Back Spread
The purchase of two or more put options at one strike price and the writing of a single put option at a higher strike price. The strike prices are selected so that the combination is delta-neutral.

Put Ratio Spread
The writing of two or more put options at one strike price and the purchase of a single put option at a higher strike price. The strike prices are selected so that the transaction is delta-neutral overall.

Putable
A derivative is putable if it can be cancelled or sold back to the issuer.

Putable Swap
See Callable Swap.

Pyramiding
The use of profits realised from an existing futures position as a new margin payment which enables the size of the position to be increased.

Quality-Spread Differential

The premium that an individual, corporation or financial institution must pay when it has a weaker credit rating compared to another individual, corporation or institution with a stronger credit rating for the same quantity of funds in the same denomination and the same maturity.

Quantity-Adjusted Currency Option

A currency option that alters during its lifetime so that it takes into account any changes in the host currency value of a financial asset. This allows a foreign currency portfolio to be hedged properly against a decline in the foreign currency even if the portfolio appreciates in value.

Quotation

The actual bid and ask price of a financial instrument at a particular time.

R

RCH
Recognised Clearing House

RCR
Registered Commodity Representative

RFC
Registered Floor Clerk

RFT
Registered Floor Trader

RIE
Recognised Investment Exchange

RLO
Restricted Life Option

ROT
Registered Options Trader

RPB
Recognised Professional Body

RSI
Relative Strength Indicator

Rainbow Option
An option that has several risk factors of the same type (such as two interest rates or three stock prices).

Random Walk Theory
See Efficient Markets.

Range Accrual Option
An option that accrues value for each period that the specified index rate stays within a specified range.

Range Binary Option
An option that pays a predetermined fixed amount upon expiry if the underlying price has stayed within a specified range for the entire option's life.

Ratchet Floater
A one-way floating rate note.

Ratio Fence
See Collar.

Ratio Hedging
Very few situations can be perfectly hedged and the changes in the price of an underlying asset will not be exactly matched by the changes in the price of the hedging instrument. This may be because the futures contract does not exactly match the item being hedged or the nature of the underlying asset differs from the notional asset on which the hedge is based. In such a situation the trader must know the ratio in which they must adjust their futures position for a given change in the underlying.

Realised Volatility
The volatility that occurred during the life of a derivatives contract that was unknown beforehand and which had to be estimated.

Receiver
The party in a Swap agreement that receives the fixed rate and pays the floating rate.

Redemption Linked Bond
A security in the form of a bond which is created with a payoff profile linking the final redemption amount to movements in an underlying equity.

Reference Bank
A bank that is used to calculate "fair" settlement values on complex derivative contracts.

Reinvestment Risk
The risk that you will not be able to reinvest money unexpectedly returned to you (perhaps through a callable bond or repayment of a mortgage backed security) at rates as favourable as those that you have been receiving.

Relative Strength Indicator
A technical analysis measure used to assess an instrument's position in the market. An RSI above 70 indicates the instrument may be overbought and an RSI below 30 indicates it may be oversold.

Relative Volatility Trading
The active trading of anomalies which occur between the volatilities of options on different (but related) assets usually caused by model differences.

Reparations
The compensation that is paid to a wronged party in a dispute over a derivatives transaction.

Replicating Portfolio
A portfolio of securities that is constructed in order to imitate the returns on a derivative security (but is much more liquid).

Repo
Short for sale-and-repurchase agreement. A contract where two parties agree for one of the parties to buy an asset spot and sell it forward at a pre-agreed price to the other party in the agreement.

Reporting Limit
The size of a position beyond which derivatives traders must make daily reports to the exchange.

Resetable Coupon
A form of bond where the issuer is allowed to reset the coupon level partway through the life of the bond.

Resetting Strike Option
An option where the strike price is set, on pre-defined dates, to a fixed percentage of the existing market level at that time.

Resistance Level
A technical analysis barrier beyond which the value of a financial instrument will not pass until breakout occurs. The opposite of support level.

Retender
The right of futures contracts holders who have been tendered a delivery notice to offer the notice for sale on the open market (thereby liquidating their obligation to take delivery).

Retractable Coupon
A form of bond which allows the investor to sell the bonds back to the issuer (at par) if the new coupon on a Resetable Coupon Bond is unacceptable.

Reversal Arbitrage
A risk-free profit created by buying a call and selling the underlying future and selling a put (a synthetic call) with the same strike price and settlement date.

Reverse Swap
A Swap between two parties with exactly opposite conditions as a Swap that has already been entered into. This is used as an alternative to selling the original Swap in order to close out a position.

Rho
A measure of the sensitivity of an option's value to interest rates. Interest rates affect the price of a derivative instrument because the cash that is represented in the deal could have been placed on deposit in the intervening period and would, itself, increased in value. Mathematically it is defined as:

$$Rho = \rho = \Delta P / \Delta R$$

Where ΔP is the change in option or portfolio value, and ΔR is the change in interest rates.

Right
A call warrant.

Ring Trading
Another term for Pit Trading.

Risk Management
The use of derivatives to control the financial risk to which an individual, corporation or institution may become exposed.

Risk Premium
An amount added to interest rates by a lender which reflects the lender's perceived ability of the borrower to repay the loan on maturity and continually service interest payments.

Risk Reversals
The purchase of an out-of-the-money put option (or call) and the sale of an out-of-the-money call option (or put) with the same maturity and amount. In a Barrier-European combination either the put or the call or both are replaced with a barrier option.

Rollercoaster Swap
A Swap where the principal is allowed to vary during the Swap's lifetime by pre-arranged amounts on pre- arranged dates.

Round Lot
A quantity of an underlying which is equal in size and type to the corresponding futures contract.

Round Turn
The purchase (or sale) of a futures contract and complimentary sale (or purchase) of an equal number of futures contracts to the same delivery month.

S

SAEF
Stock Exchange Automated Execution Facility

SAFE
1. Synthetic Agreement for Forward Exchange
2. Simulation Analysis of Financial Exposure

SAFEX
South African Futures Exchange

SDR
Special Drawing Rights

SEAQ
Stock Exchange Automated Quotation System

SES
Singapore Stock Exchange

SFA
Securities and Futures Authority

SIMEX
Singapore International Monetary Exchange

SOFFEX
Swiss Options and Financial Futures Exchange

SONIA
Sterling Overnight Interbank Average

SPAN
Standard Portfolio Analysis for Margin Requirements

SPIN
Standard & Poor's Index Notes

SQQ
Standard Quality Quotation

SWINGS
Sterling Warrants Into Guilt-Edged Securities

Sample Grade
The lowest quality of commodity acceptable for delivery of a futures contract.

Scalper
A speculator who works on an exchange trading floor and who buys and sells very quickly to make small but multiple profits. Scalpers help create market liquidity.

Screen Price
The price given on a computer screen.

Sector Risk
Similar to market risk but only covering the group of companies which are engaged in the same industrial sector.

Securitisation
The term often used to describe the conversion of a physical or financial asset into a tradable commodity.

Security
A tradable obligation.

Security Deposit
*See **Margin**.*

Segregated Account
An account used to separate customers assets from those of a broker.

Settlement Risk
The financial risk exposure incurred by an individual, corporation or institution when they have met their obligations under a contract but the counterparty has yet to do so. This includes failure by a counterparty to deliver the correct financial instrument (or to deliver it to the correct location) as well as failure to make the payments on time. The majority of settlement failures come about as a result of error rather than fraud.

Short
The sale of a derivatives contract.

Shout Option
An option where the buyer has the right at any one point during the life of the option to set the sample point at the current spot level. *See **Look Backs**.*

Single-Scenario Risk Measure
A financial risk measure which is based on estimating the outcome of one possible influence or scenario.

Special Purpose Vehicle
The combination of a bond and a derivatives trade into a single agreement.

Speculator
Someone who attempts to anticipate price fluctuations ahead of the market.

Specific Risk
The risk which is unique to an individual investment. It represents that part of an asset which is volatile and does not correlate to market movements.

Split Fee Option
A compound option (option on an option) where the purchaser makes up to three payments. The first payment initiates the agreement and the second keeps it alive whilst the third is made for the right to exercise the final option.

Spot
The price used for immediate delivery of an underlying asset.

Spot Zero Rates
Interest rates that are payable on maturity of a financial instrument with no intermediate payments.

Spread Trade
A derivatives trade that makes gains from a positive move in one financial risk factor and an opposite move in another.

Stack Hedge
The use of a block of futures contracts that mature at or around the same time in order to hedge a future exposure. Compare with Strip Hedge.

Standard Portfolio Analysis of Risk
A model used to simulate the reaction of a portfolio when exposed to extreme changes in the market. It is used as a

means for establishing margin requirements by the clearing house who need to know the largest possible intra-day loss that could be incurred by the portfolio.

Start Date
The effective date in a Swap agreement from which interest is calculated.

Stochastic
Something which evolves randomly over time.

Step-Down Coupon
A bond which initially produces a coupon above current market rates, but whose coupon is reduced on pre-specified dates in a downward direction.

Step Options
Complex products designed to provide additional gains if certain conditions occur. For example, a step-down call (or step-up put) is created by purchasing a knock-out option with a barrier at the level at which you wish the strike to improve, and a simultaneous purchase of a knock-in option with both strike and barrier at that level.

Step Payment Option
A European Option at a price which is determined in steps by the movement of the underlying price.

Step-Up Bond
A bond with a coupon that increases by pre-specified amounts on pre-specified dates. The bonds are callable at par on each of the dates set for the coupon revision.

Step-Up Coupon
A bond which begins producing a coupon below the current market rates, but which increases on pre-specified dates.

Sterling Overnight Interbank Average
An average of the interest rates paid by British brokers on overnight deposit.

Sticky Floater
A one-way floating rate note.

Stop Loss Order
An order to sell which is triggered when a specific price is reached in a downward direction. The broker must still execute at the best possible price once the trigger has been reached.

Stop Order
An order that becomes a market order when a predetermined price level is reached in specified direction. *See **Stop Loss Order***.

Straddle
The purchase of a call option and a put option on the same underlying with the same maturity and at the same strike price. The result is a strategy which benefits the purchaser if the price of the underlying proves to be volatile.

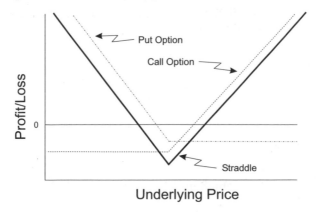

Strangle
The purchase of a call option and a put option on the same underlying for the same maturity but at a different strike price. This is a similar strategy to a straddle but requires greater volatility before it shows a profit. However the options involved are usually out-of-the-money and so is cheaper to create than a straddle.

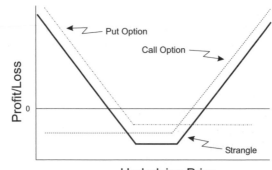

Underlying Price

Strap
A straddle plus another one of the call options.

Strike Price
The price at which the holder of an option may exercise and buy or sell the underlying.

Strip
1. A straddle plus another one of the put options.
2. A sequence of similar options but with different expiry dates.

Strip Hedge
The use of a strip of futures contracts with different maturities to hedge against a future exposure. Compare with Stack Hedge.

Structured Product
A product that is sold as a stand-alone even thought it has been created from a portfolio of other derivative products.

Stub Risk
The risk that the first contract in any futures strip will prove premature in its outlook on interest rate movements.

Support
A technical analysis level below which prices will not fall before breakout occurs. It is the point at which buyers start to outnumber sellers.

Swap
The exchange of a sequence of cashflows (usually payments) on two or more different financial instruments which has the effect of transforming one type of financial risk into another.

Swaplet
A Swap that consists of only one payment.

Swaption
An option to enter into a Swap at a specified strike rate.

Switch
The liquidation of a futures position in one delivery month and simultaneous commencement of a similar futures position in another delivery month.

Synthetic Agreements for Forward Exchange
Financial instruments used in hedging agreements which "fix Swap points" between two currencies for a pre-arranged future period.

Synthetic Convertible
The purchase of an at-the-money warrant and placement of a sum of cash into an interest bearing account. The cash placed in the account will be equal to the difference between the warrant price and the underlying share price. This strategy gives the same result as a bond which is convertible into an equity.

Synthetic Future
A synthetic long (short) is created by buying (selling) a call option and selling (buying) a put on the same future with the same strike price and the same expiry date.

Synthetic Instrument
When a derivatives instrument structure is altered in such a way as to simulate the movement of another instrument.

Synthetic Option
A synthetic put option is created by buying a call option and shorting the underlying, and a synthetic call option is created buying the underlying future and buying a put option.

Systematic Risk
Another term for market risk.

TED
T-Bond/Eurodollar Spread

TIBOR
Tokyo Interbank Offered Rate

TIFFE
Tokyo International Financial Futures Exchange

TIMS
Theoretical Indicative Margin System

TRIPS
Treasury Indexed Principal Swaps

TRS
Trade Registration System

TSE
Tokyo Stock Exchange

Tailed Calendar Spread
A calendar spread involving a long position and short position of different sizes.

Taker
The buyer of an option.

Tandem Spread
A spread made up of calendar spreads with different underlyings.

Technical Analysis
A way of predicting the movement of financial markets based on charts of historical data.

Tender
The declaration by a seller of a futures contract that they intend to delivery the physical commodity underlying the contract, and the passing on in turn by the clearing house of this declaration to the (oldest) buyer for that delivery month.

Termination
The cancellation of a derivatives agreement when allowed-for in the contract.

Theoretical Spot Rate
The rate which is used as a discounting factor in order to calculate the zero-coupon yield curve.

Theta
Measures the sensitivity of a derivative instrument with respect to time. Mathematically described as:

$$\text{Theta} = \Theta = \Delta P / \Delta T$$

Where ΔP is the change in option or portfolio value, and ΔT is the change in time.

Three-Legged Fence
See Collar.

Tick
The smallest movement allowed in the value of a derivative.

Time Decay
The fall in value of a derivative product as it approaches maturity or expiry.

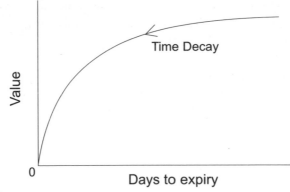

Time Value
See Extrinsic Value.

Tracking Error
A direct reflection of the active risk inherent in a particular portfolio. It is a quantification of how different the investments are from the accepted benchmark for the portfolio and shows a portfolio's managers approach.

Transaction Risk
The risk that the correct transaction or the right amount of a transaction may not be executed properly.

Trend Line
A line drawn on a chart in technical analysis that connects a sequence of highs or lows.

Triangular Arbitrage
The realisation of a risk-free profit from transactions involving three instruments.

Triple Witching Hour
The situation when settlement dates for equity options, index options and futures fall on the same day. Program trades executed on these days can cause large price swings for purely technical reasons.

To-Arrive Contract
A commodity contract where the price is based on delivery to a specified destination point, with the seller paying the freight charges.

Unauthorised Trading
The buying or selling of a derivatives contract for a customer's account without the customer's prior permission. Also includes the buying and selling of contracts contrary to employment conditions or beyond a permitted limit.

Uncovered Option
See Naked Option.

Underlying
The physical instrument, commodity, interest rate, currency or service (and even future or option) against which a future or option is traded.

Underlying Position
The fundamental position of a portfolio at any given time.

Unwind
The act of reversing an existing contract.

Up and In Option
An option that pays nothing until the underlying rises beyond a pre-determined level.

Up and Out Option
A put option that ceases to exist if the value of the underlying rises above a predetermined level.

VAR
Value at Risk

Value at Risk
Directly quantifies how much money can be made in a predefined period. It is a statistical risk measure used for a stated period and a given confidence level.

Value Date
The day on which the owner of a bond begins to accrue interest from the bond.

Variable Principal Swap
*See **Rollercoaster Swap**.*

Vega
The sensitivity of an option to the implied volatility of the underlying instrument. Also known as kappa, lambda and sigma. Described mathematically as:

$$Vega = \Sigma = \Delta P / \Delta V$$

Where ΔP is the change in option or portfolio value, and ΔV is the change of implied volatility. Other notations for Vega include Kappa (κ), Lambda (Λ) and Sigma (Σ).

Vega Trading
The buying and selling of financial instruments in order to take advantage of changes in implied volatility. *See **Volatility Trading**.*

Vertical Strategies
Trading strategies which involve the purchase and/or sale of calls or puts with the same expiry date but different exercise prices.

Vol-Vol
The "Volatility of Volatility"; which assumes that volatility is itself a random market risk factor instead of being known and constant as in the Black-Scholes model.

Volatility
One of the most popular and basic statistical measures of risk. It can be used to measure market risk for a single financial instrument, a group of instruments or even an entire portfolio. Exact definitions may vary but the most common in the financial markets is that of "standard deviation". In other words the volatility of a financial instrument is proportional as to how far its value varies from the mean.

Volatility Trading
The purchase of put and call options of the same strike and of the same maturity in order to profit from any increasing volatility of the underlying. *See* ***Straddle*** and ***Strangle***.

Volume
A measure of the level of activity in any form of derivatives contract over a given period (usually one trading day). Relative volumes give a good indication as to the validity of an instrument's value.

Vulnerable Derivatives
Derivatives which carry a risk that the writer of the derivative could default.

WI
When Issued

Warehousing
The holding of one leg of a Swap while seeking a customer whose requirements include the second leg of the Swap.

Warrant
An option issued by a company with its own shares as the underlying asset. The exercise of a warrant usually includes the issuing of new shares and therefore dilution of the company's assets. Warrants traditionally have longer times to expiry than options.

Wedding Warrant
Warrants that may only be exercised if the host bond is given up at the same time.

Whipsaw
A trader is whipsawed if the volatility of the markets, combined with stop-loss orders and limit-buying orders mean that at the end of a trading period the portfolio remains unchanged but as incurred two or more sets of transaction charges.

Window Warrant
A warrant that can only be exercised during a certain period (window).

Writer
An option seller is often called the writer.

Worst-of-Two Option
An option which pays the lower of two possible pay offs. *See **Best-of-Two Option***.

Xerxes
The derivative of a financial instrument's convexity with respect to its yield.

Yield Burning
The fraudulent activity of replacing high-yielding bonds with similarly titled low-yielding bonds in a complex derivatives agreement.

Yield Enhancement
The alteration of a pre-existing position in an effort to increase profits by exploiting favourable movements in the markets. As opposed to speculation which is the initiation of a position (where one did not exist before) to exploit market movements.

Yield Spread Option
An option whose pay-off is dependent on the size of the difference between two specified yield rates.

ZEPO
Zero Exercised Price Option

Zero Cost Collar
*See **Costless Collar**.*

Zero Coupon Bond
A bond with no intermediate cash flows or coupons and pays par at maturity.

Zero Coupon Swap
A Swap where one party incurs no intermediate cash flows and pays only a single payment at maturity but receives regular intermediate cash flows from the counterparty. Considerable credit risk is incurred by the counterparty who pays the regular cash flows.

Zero Coupon Yield Curve
The curve produced using theoretical spot rates to show yield over time.

Zero Exercised Price Option
A European call option with a strike price of zero. Since it will definitely be exercised it is the same as owning the underlying but without receiving the intermediate cash flows until expiry.

Zero Gain Collar
A costless collar made up from a short call and long put in the particular situation when the short call strike is at-the-money.